# BECOME THE GO TO BUSINESS

## For Startups

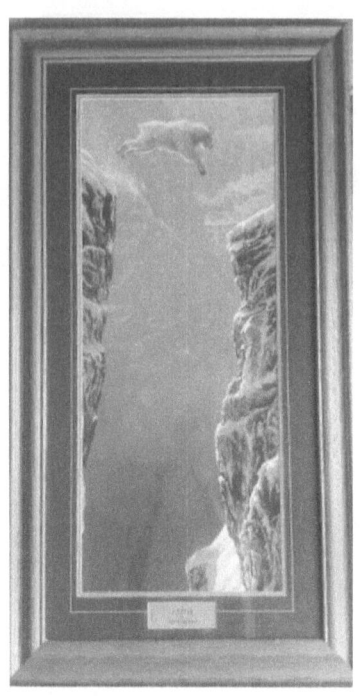

This book is dedicated to my Dad. Throughout the course of my entrepreneurial life, he always encouraged me. Prior to his passing, he bought me this picture and asked me to hang it where I would see it every day. He shared that it reminded him of the many leaps of faith he has witnessed me take. He wanted it to serve as a reminder for me to continue to be brave, encouraged, and to believe in myself.

Dad, not a day goes by that I don't see your message of faith in me. Thank you for your many gifts of wisdom and support.

## START IT RIGHT AND ACHIEVE SUCCESS

If you are reading this book, you are definitely serious about your new business (or business idea) and hungry enough to make it work. While inspiration and positive attitude are essential ingredients, this book is not a lot of "hype." This book offers real-life actions you can take to address your real-life business issues!

Have you ever noticed that motivational seminars, books, and workshops, which can offer valuable and inspirational information, often leave us feeling excited but wondering, "How do I apply that to MY situation?" That is a critical question. There is no "one size fits all" in business; however, there ARE basic principles that fit ALL business.

Not everyone's goal is to be a billionaire with a private jet. There are a lot of small business owners out there that want a comfortable life, college money for the kids and retirement. Yes, some want to be the billionaire with the private jet! Then there are the ones in between. Wherever you are and whatever your goals, let's make it happen!

The names of businesses and their owners are fictitious to protect client privacy; however, the examples offered throughout this book are real.
In addition to this book, we provide online workshops and can tailor information to meet your unique needs. You can also email us at info@mauriconsulting.com. We can serve you in many ways; sign up for our online services, including workshops, seminars, helpful tips, speaking engagements, one on one consulting, coaching and more. Go to our website:

www.mauriconsulting.com for more information. Let's take a leap of faith together!

NOTE

America is built on dreams—the dreams of people who turn their visions into reality by starting new businesses. All businesses, regardless of their focus, share common themes. They start out small and grow in size, becoming successful. This can only be accomplished with the help of the people and communities that support, encourage, and refer customers to them. Supporting small businesses strengthens communities by informing people of products and services they can trust. This creates jobs and has a positive effect on the economy. The trickle-up effect is the backbone that built this great country of the United States into the most successful country in the world.

Small business owners work hard to become successful, and most pay their employees over the minimum wage. Some also treat their employees like family. Small business offers personalized services not found in larger corporations. It is the heart of the American Dream.

# TABLE OF CONTENTS

CHAPTER 1 - -SUCCESS, WHAT DOES IT MEAN TO YOU?

CHAPTER 2 -- KNOW YOUR WHY

CHAPTER 3 --KNOW YOUR NUMBERS

CHAPTER 4 --KNOW YOUR NUMBERS-NEXT LEVEL

CHAPTER 5 -- DID YOU START YOUR BUSINESS ON THE RIGHT FOUNDATION?

CHAPTER 6 - WHY YOU SHOULD TRACK YOUR BUSINESS AND HOW

CHAPTER 7 --WHAT FEARS ARE HOLDING YOUR BUSINESS BACK

CHAPTER 8-- IS THE CUSTOMER ALWAYS RIGHT?

CHAPTER 9 – WHY YOU NEED OTHERS

# CHAPTER 1 - -SUCCESS, WHAT DOES IT MEAN TO YOU?

Success is different for everyone. For some people, it is about acquiring a certain amount of wealth. Money, to them, is the only indicator of wealth. For some people, success is about acquiring status through ownership of luxuries such as large homes, fancy cars, boats, and expensive toys. For other people, success isn't necessarily the amount of money accumulated, but what the money allows them to do. They believe that the ability to help other people have a better life and earn a good living by providing a good service is a noble endeavor. Some feel that you cannot truly be successful unless you are able to give back in some way. There is no right or wrong way to define success because your success can only be defined by you.

How I define success? Success for me is being happy, living the life I want to live, and spending time with people I love. It is also having the time, the freedom, and the money I need to serve my family and community with a huge emphasis on paying it forward. What good is money if you are too busy working to enjoy its benefits?

Think about what success means to you. What is your passion? What would REALLY make you happy?

> Do your know how to track where you are on your success journey?

Once you determine what success means to you personally, then look at your business to determine what success will look like to afford the lifestyle you desire. It could be a certain revenue goal; a certain number of employees; or who your company is and how it is perceived in the community.

For some, success is measured in the size of the company's profit. Sometimes, we believe money will make our personal lives successful. However, success in your personal life can bring success to your business. They go hand-in-hand. When you reach success milestones in your personal life, it definitely makes a difference in your business. At the same time, it takes successes in business to bring you to some of your personal successes! They are equally important.

It is time to define your success, make a plan, and track it. Where are you now? Are you at ground zero? Have you had some success or many successes? How far do you think you are from your ultimate successful lifestyle?

Here are a few things to think about while determining what your success will look like. Do materialistic things make you successful? You see, in my opinion, people are more interested in your character and the positivity you display. When you are happy and successful, it will show in YOU, not what you own. Some people think that if they have two houses or expensive cars, they will look successful, even if they are not. Do you really want to be drowning in debt so you can be perceived a certain way by others? I have seen this happen so many times. A business owner wants to portray success so that people buy from them. They have said to me,

"If I don't drive the right vehicle, they will think I am not a successful business owner and will not buy from me," or "I have to look the part in order for them to believe in me," or "I am a realtor, I must drive them around in an expensive car so they believe that I can sell houses." I have heard it all.

When I meet someone who is truly successful (and I have no clue what material things they have), I am inclined to buy from them regardless of where they live or what they drive. I have no idea how wealthy they are, but I see the energy of success they possess. That is what attracts me to buy!

Who is actually more successful in these scenarios? Someone who lives in a slightly smaller house that will be paid off soon and vehicles that are a few years old, but paid for? Or someone who has a larger house, new vehicles and is in serious debt?

I am not saying that you should not have all of the things you desire! Not at all! In fact, this book is intended to help you acquire all of those desires. What I am saying is, go with your heart, and determine what will really make YOU happy, not based on other's perceptions of your success. Want what **you** want, and do not worry about what others think you should have to appear successful.

Rome wasn't built in a day and neither will a successful business!

Time to get started. Step one is to define your ultimate successful lifestyle. Use the worksheet below to help you with that definition, using the two biggest items: time and money.

- If you had all the money you needed and did not have to work, what would you do with your time?
- What are the items on your bucket list?
- What do you want your legacy to be?
- If you had all the money and time you needed, who would you help and why?
- What would be your dream job?
- What values are important to you?
- What are your favorite things to do for fun?
- Who do you enjoy spending the most time with?
- What is your favorite hobby/pastime?
- What are ten most important items you would buy if you had the money?
- How do you want your business to be perceived by others?

Of the above 11 questions, how many of those things are you doing or have now? How much money and time would you need to acquire what you wrote on the list that you do not already have?

Calculate how much money it would take to acquire all of your desires. Include things like material items (cars, houses, etc.), as well as vacations, children's education, everything. Calculate the number on a monthly basis. Here are two worksheets to help you get started. These are just examples, which you will need to personalize for yourself.

| Current Bills | Amount |
|---|---|
| Mortgage/Rent | |
| Utilities | |
| Insurance | |
| Vehicle Payments | |
| Food | |
| Clothing | |
| Gas, vehicle maintenance | |
| Loans | |
| Credit Cards | |
| Medical (insurance & expenses) | |
| Children's activities/school or daycare tuition/child support/alimony | |
| Add in Taxes/household upkeep/personal upkeep (gym, nails, haircuts, etc.), pets, entertainment, giving (tithes, gifts/donations), and add a savings goal maybe? | |
| Total Monthly Expense | |

| Desired Items | Cost Per Month to Acquire |
|---|---|
| New Vehicle | |
| Home/Second Home | |
| Recreational Vehicles | |
| Travel (vacations) | |
| Hobbies/Activities | |
| Memberships | |
| | |
| Total Monthly Expense | |

We will define the amount of money you will need for your desired lifestyle here. You will need that number when you get to the chapter "Know Your Numbers."

First, write down your current bills per month. Research the cost of your desired interests, purchases, etc. Include everything and break it down to a monthly amount.

Add the total of both worksheets to acquire the total amount you would need each month to keep what you have and add your lifestyle desires.

Next, figure out how many hours a month you want to devote to the activities you enjoy.

Here is a little guide to help you. This is based on a week, in which there are 168 total hours. We have put some examples in to help you. You can create your own as it fits your activities. Do two worksheets—one based on your current lifestyle and one based on your desired lifestyle.

| Desired Activities & Required Activities | Hours |
|---|---|
| Sleep (how many hours do you get or want) | |
| Family Time | |
| Exercise | |
| Hobby/Interest | |
| Me Time (Things you do just for you. Maybe getting a massage!) | |
| Work | |
| | |
| | |
| | |

After filling out the current and desired worksheets, there may be a difference. You may have more hours needed than there are in a week. At this point, you most likely will not have enough hours in the week for all required and desired activities. These worksheets are defining where you are now and where you want to be. How many more hours a week do you need? How many hours of work would you have to cut back for the other activities? Your time required for your success is now calculated; now it is time to work on your business to achieve your success.

Keep in mind, this is all about where you are now and where you want to be. Your definition of success may change as you achieve your goals. It may also change after a major life event, such as marriage, birth of a child, etc.
Now, you know what will make you successful and how much time and money you need to reach that success.

Start visualizing that success! Picture in your mind what your life would look like if you had everything on your worksheets. Keep track of it. Set reasonable timeframes for your goals.

Do a worksheet with all of the things you want to accomplish with goal dates. Put that sheet where you can see it on a daily basis. Take your worksheet where you calculated how much money you need and put that where you can see it every day! In the chapter "Know Your Numbers," you will learn what you need to do in your business to make the money for your successful lifestyle. Make sure to keep your eyes on the prize! Keep your focus on what you need to do in your business to create the lifestyle you desire.

Your passion and your why will keep you focused. Also, focus on serving others and not the money. When you focus on your dreams and serving others to achieve their dreams rather than focusing on money, your business will soar! Too much focus on money creates negativity which stifles your business and dreams.

## CHAPTER 2 -- KNOW YOUR WHY

People go into business for many reasons. Your "Why" is extremely important. So, think about this, I mean *really* think about this. Why do you want to start a business? Why did you start your business?
- Was it so you don't have to work for a boss?
- Was it because you were tired of your time off being decided by those who had more seniority?
- Was it because you had a true passion for the product/service you provide and want to help people?
- Was it because your creativity was capped or stifled?

---

*People who have not discovered their passion will lose motivation, which in turn may stifle their goals and dreams.*

---

More questions to ask yourself why you started or want to start your business:
- What makes you come alive?
- What brings fulfillment to you?
- What are some of the things you love the most?
- What are your strengths and best skills?
- How can you use those to make an impact and add value to your life and the lives of others?

Use the answers to these questions to get started.

This is starting at the end and working your way to the beginning. Do not focus on the *how* at this point, only the *why*. Once you define your true goals and dreams, we will work on the how!

Once you know your true why, SHARE IT! Your why is your story. Your why is REAL. Your story and realism will not only be easy to share with others, but it will show how genuine you are. People will see that you are not out just to make a paycheck! You have a purpose!

Sharing your *why* with your employees and customers will steer your business in the right direction.

You can share your *why* everywhere: networking groups, conversations at gatherings with family and friends. Share your *why* with strangers in an elevator!

When I share my *why* with people, my excitement shows and the people around me feel my passion. Seeing the excitement, they realize that I truly am passionate and real. It is contagious! They start getting excited for me and the more they do that, the more they go out of their way to help me achieve my dreams.

When I am around someone who is passionate about what they do, I can't help but to want to be a part of it! I want them to achieve their dreams!

Your *why* inspires you to take ACTION and it inspires others to take action also. They buy your product or service and refer you to their friends and family.

Are you working for your dreams or just money? If money is all you are looking for, you may be disappointed quickly. In most businesses, the money doesn't start coming in on day one. If money is your only desire, then you will probably lose momentum real fast. Working for your passion far outweighs working for money because it is much more fulfilling!

No matter how long you have been in business, it is not too late to dig deep and find your true *why* and start sharing it with everyone. Your *why* can change. Goals and dreams change due to life changes, i.e., marriage, children, divorce, age and so on. It is important to keep your *why* in focus and make the necessary changes as life changes.

Here are scenarios I have worked through with businesses regarding their *why*. We will walk through them and explain the importance of the *why*.

John, who owns "John's Construction", said his *why* is that he was tired of working hard to make his boss all the money. Tired of working for his boss, John complained that his boss didn't do any of the "real" work and that, if it weren't for him (John), his boss would not even have a business. Yes, John was a skilled carpenter and, of course he made his boss money. And yes, it is true that without great employees, your business cannot be successful.

John decided to leave and start his own company with the idea that he would make all the money and not have to provide someone else the great lifestyle his boss *seemed* to have. John said he had been doing all kinds of jobs on the side and made more money than what he made at his job. He believed he could make substantially more money, as well as keeping all of the money.

Unfortunately, John woke up to a much different scenario. He came to us seeking help for his business because he was seriously struggling. He was not making enough money to pay himself and take care of his family. As a business coach, my first question to him was why he went into the business. I will never deny someone the choice of their *why*. Who am I to decide? His *why*, however, was misguided and negative. It was keeping his business from moving forward. That, along with not having started his business on the right foundation caused his business to suffer.

Let's take a closer look at this particular situation. John "felt" that he made all the money for his boss and he deserved to make the money for himself. OK, that may be a valid feeling, however, it isn't exactly true. John has every right to make his dreams come true, and if his dream was owning his own business, then more power to him. I want to help him succeed. The issue is that John used his "feelings" to get him started and did not do his due diligence. Actually, jealousy played a huge part in his decision to start his own company. In my opinion, jealousy is the biggest waste of life I can think of. Remember, if you want what someone else has, then you have to accept the whole package. In other words, you need to take a closer look at what they really have (all of it, not just the material things, or what "looks" great on the "outside"). What did they do to get what they have? Where are they really? Have they fulfilled the dreams YOU want? This is about you and your dreams, not someone else's.

Instead of doing his due diligence and really watching and learning from his boss, i.e., asking him questions about the business, doing research on how to start, finding a mentor or business coach, he just quit his job and started up his business. He *assumed* that, in his former job, he was the one making all the money and the boss really didn't do anything. Whoa! John couldn't have been more wrong. Let's take a look at a construction company and what is involved. One of my many businesses happened to be a construction company, so this was an easy one for me diagnose.

A lot of employees in the construction business feel the same way John felt—that they make all the money for their bosses. I have experienced it myself with employees over the years. Let's dive in and see what it takes to be successful in this industry. The owner of a construction company has to establish the company, just like any other business. Then the real work begins. First, they need to make sure the business is set up with all the correct licensing, insurance, employees, vendors for materials, and much more. They need to find customers. They need to make sure jobs are done according to the customers' needs and in compliance with local and state laws. The building and construction industry has an entire book of codes that need to be followed. Along with that, there are many rules for licensing (each state is different). The construction business owner needs to collect the money and pay the overhead. They need to manage collections when customers don't pay on time. They need to deal with any mistakes the employees make, and the list goes on! Just because they are not swinging a hammer beside you doesn't mean they are not working their tails off! In fact, they are probably working when you are sleeping! If they have had the business for many years, their business may be at a point where they are large enough and things are running well, they don't have to eat, sleep and breathe the business. They may be off on vacations, while you are working. But it took many years of blood, sweat, and tears to reach that level.

There are so many misconceptions going on here. Let's look at those "side jobs." John may have made a lot of money from side jobs, but of course, he wasn't doing it as a real business. Side jobs give some people the impression that they will make more money working for themselves rather than working for "the man." That can totally be true, but you have to be realistic. You have to work it right first—the money will come later, sometimes much later. Like I said, I am totally pro small businesses, but it needs to be done correctly.

If you are in a job similar to John's, (construction is not the only type of business that has "side jobs"), then here are some questions to ask yourself before going into business:
- How many side jobs will you have coming in and from who?
- How long will jobs from your friends and family keep you going until you have to start looking for more work?
- Will your current side job customers pay the higher prices you will have to charge when you have that legitimate business set up?

John needed to consider the fact that prices will need to go up because of overhead. Even if he didn't rent a space somewhere or buy a building, he would have overhead including insurances, licenses, payroll taxes, advertising and more

Another point missed by John was that employees *do* make a business owner money—that is the point of hiring them. If an employee doesn't make you money, then why would you hire them? Yes, there are some employees in a business who do not actually generate money because their positions are necessary to keep the company going. But the majority of the employees should be making money for the company.

So, now what to do about John? Well, first of all, John needed to get up to speed on what it really takes to become a successful contractor. The very first order of business was for him to change his mindset and realize his true *why*. After much thinking, he realized that his real *why* was that he did not want to be held back in any way. He wanted to be able to go as high in his industry as possible and not be capped on the amount of money he could make. He felt that if the sky was the limit, he could be a much better provider for his family and be much happier with himself and his work. His main goals were about his children. He wanted them to be able to participate in all of the activities they wanted and to have a college fund for them. He was also concerned about retirement. Construction is very hard on the body and he had no idea how long he would be able to do this work. Because of that, he needed a plan in place for when he could no longer do the physical labor. He wanted a business that could run without him doing the actual work someday. Now, there is a *why* we could really work with.

First, he defined what true success was to him. Then he used his *why* to drive him to his success. He visualized on a daily basis what life would look like when he had enough money and time to achieve his dreams. He wrote down these goals and dreams and kept them where he could see them frequently throughout the day. Seeing these goals and dreams every day drove him in the right direction! He tracked his successes one by one. As he started to see each goal achieved, he became even more excited and more driven!

We worked with him on everything you will be reading about in this book including John determining his definition of success and his *why*. He set goals and dates for achieving goals. He calculated his numbers so he knew how to get revenue flowing into his business to meet those goals. John had not started his business on the right footing, so we worked with him to fix those issues and got him on track. We set up strategic marketing plans, tracked his business, and so on. As you read on, you will see that John had a lot to do. But now his business is now thriving and he is living his dream.

The reason your *why* is SO important is because that is what drives you!!! To be successful, you need drive. John was missing the drive because his *why* was negatively-based. It was based on jealousy. Your why will drive you big-time. His original *why* was driving him right into the ground. His new *why* is now allowing him to make appropriate changes and he is now soaring in his business!

John also had to look at his mindset about employees and about making "other people" money. That was a huge step, but it made a huge positive change. He had to realize that he also needed to have employees who made him money. Another reality for his industry, especially because he was starting small, was that he needed to be open to work for other contractors. I say "needed to be **open**," not that he had to do this, but to be open to the idea. Once he understood that in order to get more work, he may have to subcontract from larger contractors and they would make money off of his efforts, he got it! It was a great experience to watch his mindset change and his business turn around. Once he got rid of the chip on his shoulder of working for "the man" and making other people money, he took on some subcontract work and it propelled his business. He actually enjoyed the fact that the larger contractors were making money from his work! He was starting to have a more *pay it forward* and serving mentality. This new mentality encouraged him even more.

He brought in the money he needed to grow the business. Eventually, he was hiring subcontractors for his now much larger construction company. He is not swinging a hammer anymore and is only working on the vision of his company. His change of mindset and business practice has made John become successful. He is also telling his employees what he learned so they don't jump to the conclusions he did. On top of that, he is training the ones who are interested, to become business owners themselves one day! What a *pay it forward* guy! Go John!!

Let's look at another real-life example of a why. "Mary," we will call her, was unhappy at her job because she was a free spirit and a bit of a rebel. Mary hated the fact that she had to follow so many rules and regulations and did not have a voice in her job about how things should be done. She felt like she was in a cage in all respects: like how much money she could make, how creative she could be, when she could and could not take time off of work and so on.

Her father-in-law got very sick and she took time off so she and her husband could go see him. Her husband's father lived on the other side of the country in a remote area. The one and only airline in that town was on strike, so they drove. They were gone seven days. Four days after they returned, Mary's father-in-law passed away.

Mary went to her boss and said she needed to take off another week to go to the funeral. The airlines were still on strike and they would have to drive. Mary's boss said, "No, you can't leave again." Mary said, "I will take it without pay, but I have to go." Her boss replied, "It is not YOUR father, so why do you need to go?" That was the last straw.

The employer here really lost out. A little bit about Mary's past: Mary had several jobs and in each one she gave 100% effort to the company. She worked hard to help the companies she worked for grow and prosper. Mary had tons of great ideas that would have brought in more revenue, and she had ideas about areas where money could be saved. Unfortunately, most of her bosses thought that, because of her age, she didn't know anything; they would not listen. They told her there was no way she could know more than they did about how to grow *their* business. If this boss would have listened more and paid attention and been a little more flexible, he would have had a wonderful asset to his business for years to come. Instead, his ego and bossiness led to losing a great employee.

Mary decided that no one should ever tell her who is important in her life and whose funeral she should or should not attend. She decided it was time to do her own thing and soon. Mary made a plan. She decided to start her own business. She believed that, in nine months, her business would be in a position to allow her to quit her job. She chose a business that was right up her alley! It was a business that did not require her to be in an office all day, or that stifled her creativity; she could make visions happen. She also decided that someday when she had employees, she was not going to be like prior bosses she had. Mary decided she was going to be a leader rather than a boss.

Mary was determined. While still at her job, she worked diligently in her free time to get her business started.

She went to networking groups in the morning before going to work and on her lunch hour, along with spending evenings and weekends working on her business. She did her due diligence to start the business out on the right foot. She wrote out her vision and goals and how she planned on getting there. This took a lot of hard work, but she was determined. Her *why* is what was gave her the necessary drive and determination. She was focused on why. That is so important because you can focus on your goals all day long, but the reason why you want those goals is so much stronger than anything. It gives you the energy and excitement you need to make it happen. The *why* is your purpose for doing it. The more important your *why* is to you, the more drive you will experience. You have to have strategies to get to the goals, but if you don't know your real *why*, you will never reach your highest potential.

Mary's *why* was to be able to be the free spirit she is, be happy, and make a living. Her true "why" was because she wanted to control her own life, creativity, and bank account. Mary focused every day on freedom of creativity, control of her bank account, and time freedom she planned to acquire with her new business. Mary created a vision board filled with what her new life would look like. She kept her vision board where she could look at it every day to positively help her move forward, rather than paying attention to the negative environment of her job. Interestingly enough, in the first few years, she worked way more hours than she ever did at her job. Instead of the 9-5 hours required by her job, she was working from 7:00 am to anywhere from 6:00 pm to 10:00 pm! It was her choice to work those hours, not anyone else and she loved every single minute of it! Mary's business was run Mary's way and she enjoyed her business so much, she didn't feel like she was working at all. Mary became extremely successful! It all started with the drive for her "why".

What is your *why*? Dig deep, because your *why* isn't always what you really think it is. Make sure your why is a very positive one and then drive it to success!

Sharing about Mary is not just about how her *why* drove her to her successful business, but also a lesson on how to treat employees. There will be more on that in a later chapter.

Write down your *why*. If you can find pictures that depict your *why*, put them on a board where you can see them every day. Keep your *why* in focus at all times, because it will drive you to your goals. Remember to share your *why* with your employees, mentors, coaches, colleagues, customers—everyone!

Getting to your goals is easier when you help others get to their goals. Here is a good start. Have a meeting with all of your employees. You can do this as a group or individually.

Ask your employees what their goals and dreams are and find out their *why*. Make sure they give you true *why's*. Don't just accept the answer, "Well, I want to make a lot of money." Keep asking why, until they tell you the deep true reason they want to make money. Ask them what they think would be success for them. It can be very easy to incorporate your employees' goals with yours.

If an employee's goal is to have a higher position in the company, train him or her to achieve that goal. This will help your business as it grows because they will be taking some of your duties so that you have time to work **on** the business more than **in** it. Knowing what they want helps you on so many levels. You may have a great employee who is working there just to make money so that someday they can have their dream job or open their own business.

It can be hard sometimes to think about spending a lot of time on certain employees when you know some day they are going to leave. Be a *pay it forward* business owner! If they want to have a better career and/or do something they love, schedule them so they may go to school or take some type of training. Be a mentor. If they want to be a business owner someday, teach them what you know about business and encourage them! You get what you give in this life! When they leave to pursue their dreams, someone else will come along for you to hire for that position. When I see business owners work with their employees to achieve dreams, I am way more likely to do business with them.

A business owner I know, "Maggie," has an employee who has been with her for years. This employee, "Tina," is an asset to the company. However, Tina has been working on her own business for a long time and someday wants to achieve her dreams with her business.  Maggie is mentoring Tina and training her on business ownership!  I asked Maggie if she was worried about Tina leaving.  She said, "It will be hard someday when she leaves, as she is one of my best employees and has been here so many years, but I truly love the idea of helping someone else succeed like I have."  Awesome!  Be a Maggie!  I know great things will come back to Maggie for her *pay it forward* attitude!

There are so many more examples, certainly ones that fit you.  Do you need help digging out your true *why* and how to create the drive to become successful? If you need help with that, make sure you contact us, as we can help you!

Ok, between the chapter Success and this chapter, hopefully you will know your passion, your *why* and the success you are going after.  Now, let's move onto the next chapter, "Know Your Numbers."  This is the next step to prepare you to achieve your successful lifestyle.   Too redundant.

## CHAPTER 3 --KNOW YOUR NUMBERS

A very important key to a successful business is knowing your numbers. Are you thinking of starting a business, have a new startup, or have been in business for years? Regardless of where you are, do you really know all of your numbers?

> *Many business owners do not have a handle on their numbers.*

After years of working with businesses, I have found that many business owners do not really have a handle on their numbers. Being a numbers person, I must admit that this really drives me crazy! Almost every single business owner that I have asked, says "Yes, I know all of my numbers." After we go through a session on Know Your Numbers, they find out that they don't know all of their numbers. Just recently, I asked a man who is getting ready to open up a business, "Do you know your numbers?" He said, "Yes, definitely!" Then I asked him what his numbers were. He gave me two numbers. He said, "Well, it will cost about $2000 a month to make $20,000 worth of product." That was it. Those were his numbers. I cringed again. It pains me to see so many people start out their business this way because nine times out of ten, they are either going to fail or desperately try to hang on to their business. You need to know ALL of the numbers. You also have to have a strategy. How are you going to sell the $20,000 worth of product you manufacture? He thought people were just going to buy it. Not only that, but the $2000 is just the cost of manufacturing the product. No overhead is included in this number. At this point, I didn't even know what his overhead was. This is a new client, and he is currently going through our program. I want his business to become successful.

Some small business owners have become successful, somehow, without knowing their numbers, but that is definitely not the norm. To know your numbers, you really have to get into the details of all costs, income, etc. There are so many hidden costs in business that even seasoned business owners may not think about or notice.

Why is it so important to know your numbers? You need to know your numbers so that you are in control of your business. You need to know if you are profitable or not. How can you plan for the future, i.e. starting a business, growing the business, taking the business to the level you desire, if you don't know where you are today? Taking a close look at all expenses will show you where you may be losing money, or where you may save money, or even where you may make more money. Working with small business owners, some have not had a clue they were losing money, however, some knew they were losing "a little money" and said, "Oh well, it's not that much money, I am not going to worry about it." The "little money" can add up to a lot of money over time. You may not be worried about it, but that could be an employee's bonus or raise going down the drain or maybe the loss of acquiring new equipment. To start, you need to know all of the expenses and costs of your business. One of these costs is the amount you need for your lifestyle. In the chapter, Success, you have already calculated that number.

Below is a worksheet to get you started.

## Business Expense Worksheet:

| Expense | Amount |
|---|---|
| Rent/Mortgage of business space | |
| Utilities (heat, lights, phone, alarm system, water, sewer, internet etc.) | |
| Vehicles (payments, insurance, gas, maintenance and/or mileage) | |
| Signage | |
| Marketing/Advertising | |
| Office Supplies | |
| Maintenance of building(s) | |
| Employees (wages, employment taxes, workers comp, liability insurance, unemployment taxes, health insurance, sick leave, vacation, training time, overtime, etc.) | |
| Licenses, Subscriptions, Dues, Continuing Education | |
| Insurances i.e. liability, health, disability, (some professions have different insurance requirements, i.e. malpractice, etc.) | |
| Taxes | |
| Credit Card Fees/Bank Fees/Interest/Late Fees/Miscellaneous Charges | |
| Professional Fees (CPA, Attorney, etc.) | |
| Equipment and Equipment Maintenance | |
| | |
| | |
| | |
| | |
| | |
| YOUR TIME/Lifestyle requirement | |

This list does not include every expense a business can have, this is just the list of common business expenses. Look at all of your bills coming in and add ones you don't see on the above worksheet. Let's go through some of them and take a closer look.

Rent/Mortgage. Some business owners own their buildings. Unless it is paid off, there is a mortgage. Whether paid off or not, there will always be insurance and taxes and maintenance on the building, including parking lot, snow removal (depending on where you live), possible mowing, plant maintenance, and the list goes on. If you rent the space for your business, you may have a lease that has an escalator, which means every year your rent will go up by a percentage. There may also be what is called CAM (common area maintenance). Be sure to calculate every single dollar of what either costs you and will cost you over the next year. Some CAM's vary from year to year, depending on what maintenance is needed, as well as the weather (snow removal). Always plan for CAM to go up and use the highest amount for your budgeting purposes. It would even be a good idea to ask the landlord what to expect.

Utilities. A lot of times, business owners don't pay attention to utilities. They are certainly necessary! Think about how hard it would be to do business with no electric, phone, or internet! You can only control them to a point, as you want your customers and employees to be comfortable, but it is important to do a good job keeping an eye on what they all cost, especially during different seasons. You may pay $100 per month in certain months for electricity, but $300 in extremely hot or cold months. If you are not prepared to pay the higher amounts in the higher seasons, your budget could run at a deficit.

Vehicle expenses is one area that some business owners don't calculate in their budgets. Maybe it's because insurance is generally paid every six months, not monthly. Or maybe gas and maintenance are put on credit cards and not watched closely. You need to calculate every bit of the vehicle expenses, as that is money going out of your business, in order to know if you are profiting or not, or making the profit you desire. Remember, gas, oil, oil changes, repairs, payments, insurance, all of it, needs to be calculated. If your business does not own a vehicle, then your company should be paying you mileage to use your vehicle. You should be paying mileage for every single mile that is business-related and use that number for your vehicle expenses.

Signage. This is one thing that a lot of business owners don't even think of until they try to open their business! You need a sign! Signs are not cheap, and they require maintenance. Signs can have lights, they can fade, and they can break, so you need to think about the sign whether you own the building or not.

Marketing and Advertising. This is an interesting area because some people do not know what they should do for their particular business for marketing and advertising. Marketing and Advertising is not a one size fits all proposition. You really should check out our Marketing and Advertising Workshop for that! For now, remember that everything you do in this regard is an expense. From business cards to brochures, to your website and networking groups. Every group you join that costs money, mileage to get there, the cards you hand out, ads you put in a local coupon book, radio, tv, and whatever else you are paying for to get your business out there needs to be included in your budget.

Office Supplies. We all have them—from pens and paper to toilet paper! Remember to look at what you are spending on every item used in your business and calculate how much you will be spending on a monthly basis.

Employees. I had a client who was struggling in her business. Her first complaint was, "I had no idea I had to pay employment taxes on my employees. I just can't believe I have to pay that. I can't afford it." She knew nothing about owning a business. A business was for sale, so she bought it and said, "I am a business owner." She had always been an employee. Most employees have no idea what the employer has to pay with regard to their paychecks. The employee has federal and state taxes withheld and pay a percentage of FICA. The employer takes that withholding and sends it to the appropriate agencies. However, the employer is required to match the FICA, along with paying unemployment taxes, and depending on the state, other state taxes. Not to mention workers comp, liability insurance, health insurance (in some cases), disability insurance (in some cases) and other fees and taxes. Each state has different laws and taxes to pay.

When you calculate your employee's wages when doing job costing, you have to calculate in all of the costs associated with that employee! They may make $20.00 per hour, but you may actually be spending as much as $30.00 or more per hour for that employee. If you have a business where you bill out the employee's time, it is critical to get all of this calculated and make sure you are charging enough to cover it all. Remember to calculate the time it takes to do payroll also. If you do your own payroll, you can take the amount of time it takes to do the payroll and divide by the number of your employees to get a cost per employee. The same goes if you pay someone to do your payroll. Take the amount charged and divide by the number of employees.

One of the biggest expenses business owners miss in their numbers calculation is very often regarding employees. Countless times, I have worked with business owners who use the employee's actual wage per hour to calculate time charged to the customer and then wonder why they are not making any money. It is because they might be off by anywhere from $5.00-$20.00 per hour! Think about health insurance for your employees? Figure that monthly amount divided by their hours worked, it can really add up, just like FICA, unemployment and workers comp!

Licenses/Subscriptions/Dues. These fees add up. Your business may need a business license, a professional license, or both. Your business may need to pay for certain subscriptions and/or dues. These may be small or large but are still expenses that need to be calculated for your bottom-line expenses.

Insurances. Wow, talk about not a one size fits all category. There are many different insurances for different businesses and it varies from location to location. Some of the insurances you may have to buy include liability, vehicle insurance, disability insurance, malpractice, and others.

Taxes. The type of business entity you choose (sole proprietor, LLC, Corp, S-Corp, Partnership) determines how you pay taxes on your income and the business income. There are also other taxes to consider. Some localities have a business tax they assess on your revenue or other taxes for your business. Most states have sales tax. Sales tax is generally passed on to the customer. Keep in mind though, when you see an amount per month for your revenue, some of that money is pass-through and not yours to keep. I have had clients that somehow were not paying attention to that. They would see $10,000.00 coming into the bank and forget that right off the top 6% (in their state) was not theirs to spend.

Credit Card/Bank Fees/Interest Fees/Late Fees/Misc. Fees. The same goes for credit card fees as with sales tax. The business owner sees all that money coming in and might forget that a percentage of that will be taken right back out of the account and go to the credit card company. It is something to always be thinking about when looking at revenue coming in. You will calculate your monthly operating expenses, but there will be per sale variables, such as sales taxes and credit card fees that are not going to necessarily be in your monthly budget due to variance. Remember, when you see that money coming in, to calculate the percentage that does not go into your business at all for paying operating expenses; it just isn't yours to begin with. Bank fees generally are the same every month, if you have them. However, NSF checks and check orders, or a request to the bank for documents can all cost money.

Equipment and Maintenance. This is one often overlooked item, not the equipment, but the maintenance. Keep track of what it costs to repair and maintain everything in your business.

Now the biggest one that gets overlooked by the majority of my clients! YOUR TIME/LIFESTYLE REQUIREMENTS. Yes, your time. I see business owners constantly ignoring the value of their time. They are not costing their own time, hard hours they have worked, and adding them into the business expenses. If it takes you time to do anything on, in, and for your business, there is a monetary value to it. Always put a value on your time. Yes, you will have a salary and most likely be under the employee section of the expenses. However, you have to make sure you are valuing all of your time. Maybe you need a raise!

There are small business owners that are not making enough money to pay themselves at all. In our chapter, "Did You Start Your Business on the Right Foundation" we discuss that you need a plan for your personal finances when the business is not making enough money for you to receive a paycheck. Many businesses have ups and downs, good and bad "seasons." For example, a carwash may not be as busy in January as it is in July. You must prepare for those bad seasons. During the high revenue seasons, plan to put enough money away to keep you going in the low revenue seasons.

Once you value your time, there are some decisions to make regarding that time. For example, if you can be out in the field generating thousands of dollars in revenue for your company in a one-hour meeting, why are you spending that hour doing work you could pay someone $15.00 an hour to do? Or why are you spending countless hours trying to learn how to be a CPA, attorney, bookkeeper, and human resource person? Evaluate the cost of your time and revenue lost when you are not working on the skills you have that are best for your company. Compare the revenue you would earn to the price of some of these tasks you could hire out. Are you really saving money or are you losing money, along with your sanity and time you could be spending with your family?

When calculating your numbers, keep in mind returns, losses and collections. If your business is product-based and typically has returns, you must calculate the average returns. One month you may have $20,000 in revenue and the next month $4,000 of it could be returned and now you only have $16,000 for that month. It is important to remember this so you do not spend the money you received too quickly and are unable to refund your customers. One thing to note, if you have never been in business. Credit card companies take the money right out of your checking account immediately, whether it is a return or a purchase dispute. You must keep enough money in your bank account for possible returns and disputes. Many credit card processors do not refund you the processing fee because it is a service fee for a service which was performed. A customer will get all of their money back, but depending on your card processing company, you may still be out the original fee.

Now that your operating expenses are calculated, let's look at the next action step. Calculate what your product and/or service costs and what you are charging for that product/service.

If you are just starting a business, you will need to figure out how much to charge for your product or service. If you have been in business for a while, use what you are currently charging for your product/services.

What is your profit from your products/services? Take the expenses for a month and divide that number by the amount of profit from your product or service. What is the number? That is the amount of product/service you need to sell in order to pay your expenses. Remember the pesky little things like sales tax and credit card fees!

**Example:**
Monthly expenses total: $22,000. Your average sale is $154.00 (not counting sales tax and credit card fees) and you are running at a 45% markup; your **profit** per sale (not including sales tax or credit card fees) is $84.70. You will need 260 sales to make the monthly expenses. Keep in mind, I said "profit," not revenue. It only takes 143 customers to get revenue of $22,000, but that will not pay your expenses! What you will need in revenue to get your $22,000 per month will be $40,000. To calculate monthly **revenue**: Take your total expense number and divide by the percentage of your markup.

**Example:**
You have a 45% mark up. $22,000 divided by .55 = $40,000. This is the revenue number you need to bring in to get your $22,000. The reason I do not have credit card or sales tax figured in is that every locality charges different sales tax or no sales tax, and credit card processing fees vary. Take those sales tax and credit card fees and add to the $40,000, for the total revenue. Example: If your credit card fees and sales tax = 9%, divide 40,000 by .91 and you will get the number $43,956.04. However, a lot of businesses still take checks and cash, so that number will never be 100% accurate, but it is a great number to use since it is the worst case scenario.
One thing I have noticed in working with small business owners, even ones who have been in business for 20 years, is

that they do not conduct their business on a percentage basis. To me, this is so critical. I have seen everything from, we just charge $1.00 per square foot over cost, to we do the work for the price we think we can get in our market, etc.

Running your business on a percentage basis makes it extremely easy to know your numbers on a daily basis! For example, if you run your business on a 45% markup when you look at the total receipts for the day and they are $1500.00, you just take $1500.00 and multiply by 45%, along with sales tax and credit card fees, and you will know your profit for the day. It is also easier to calculate the amount you should be charging for your products/services. If you don't know what percentage to use, you can ask vendors and check to see what the going rate is in your industry and your locality. It also makes it easier to run sales. If you are at a 45% markup, you certainly don't want to mark everything half off, you would go in the hole fast! You know that if you mark something down 10%, you will still get 35%. If you do that, remember you will need to calculate how many more sales you need to acquire your monthly revenue goal to cover all expenses. For your businesses that require estimates to customers, the percentage basis makes preparing your estimates much quicker and easier.

Remember, the revenue is the total amount of money you bring in per month, the profit of the product/service is the difference between what it cost and what you charged. The difference between the cost and what you charge (your per product/service profit) is what you need to use to pay all of your expenses. Any extra money after all expenses are paid are profit in the company. Note that your total monthly expense number used above includes the lifestyle you want, but do not yet have. You can change that number to the amount you absolutely have to make in order to survive. That will tell you where you need to be today. I have worked with business owners who see the $22,000 coming in think they are ok, but they are not, because all of the expenses have not been paid.

So, right now, how many sales do you need to break even and how much are you selling? If you are short, how many more sales do you need? If you are breaking even, how many do you need to make a profit for the business? If you are making a good profit, how many do you need to sell to get to the next level?

# CHAPTER 4 --KNOW YOUR NUMBERS-NEXT LEVEL

The formula for getting to the next level is simple. How much money do you need for the next level? First, what is your next level? Hiring more employees? Paying yourself more? Buying a building instead of renting? Expanding the business? Whatever your next desired level, calculate what the expenses would be to get there. Take that number and divide by average profit per sale.

Below is a worksheet to help you calculate the amount of sales you need, along with how many prospective customers you will need.

| 1a | Revenue needed per year | (#1) | |
|----|---|---|---|
| 1b | Average revenue per sale/transaction | (#1a) | |
| 2 | Divide revenue needed by the average revenue per sale/transaction, which will equal the number of deals you need:<br>_____ (#1) ÷ _____ (#1a) = (#2)<br>_____ (**deals needed**) | (#2) | |
| 3 | Make a reasonable estimate of your closing ratio:<br>Closing ratio of \_\_\_\_\_ out of \_\_\_\_\_ or (#3)<br>\_\_\_\_\_ % | (#3) | |
| 4 | Divide the number of deals needed per year by your closing ratio:<br>\_\_\_\_ deals you need (#2) ÷ _____ closing ratio (#3) = (#4) _____<br>This is the number of **Prospects Needed** | (#4) | |
| 5 | Determine how many deals are currently being worked on and subtract the number you have from the number you need (#4) | | |

|   |   |   |   |
|---|---|---|---|
|   | Prospects that need to be added for the year | (#5) |   |
| 6 | Divide (#5) by the number of weeks you plan on working this year |   |   |
| 7 | This number equals the number of NEW PROSPECTS per week you need to add to keep up with your goal. |   |   |
| 8 | Make a reasonable estimate of the time it takes to close a deal.<br>Average lead-time to close each deal is _____ weeks |   |   |
| 9 | 52 weeks ÷ _____ weeks needed to close deal = estimated deal turnover time<br>_____ |   |   |
| 10 | Divide this estimate into the total number of deals needed. This equals the number of deals needed in your "currently working with" prospect pool at all times.<br>_____ Deals (#4) ÷ _____ (#5) = _____<br>Deals you need currently at all times. |   |   |

All of the above may seem so basic to you if you have gone through this before. However, I often see people who have been in business for years who have learned something about their businesses by doing this because they have never done it before. They realized that they had not been calculating all of the costs and were losing money because of it, or not understanding why they were not getting ahead. Once they realized it and together we made some changes, they soared to the next level! This is also a book for everyone, including beginners who may have never seen any of this. My goal is to serve everyone I possibly can!

More hidden costs. Do you have employees? Are they late, do they leave early, do they take long lunches? All of this matters. You may not think so on a daily or weekly basis, but let's do some real numbers.

My clients, Louise and Ken, had an employee who showed up 15 minutes late every day. Occasionally, like once a week, she took 15 extra minutes for lunch, oh and she was notorious for leaving early, like 5-15 minutes before closing three times a week (thinking it was slow, so it was ok). The worst part is that she was in charge of opening and closing the business. A customer would show up at 4:45 and find locked doors displaying a sign that says *open until 5:00*. They drove all the way there just to see the business closed early for no apparent reason. Will they come back? Who knows. There have been times when I have gone to a business during what they say is their "normal" business hours and no one was there. No sign saying "back in 5 minutes." Just closed. I will just go to the next business that is open! Time is very precious! I no longer want to waste precious time waiting for people to show up or go to a business where they closed a half-hour early. I will just take my business elsewhere!

Let's calculate what this is costing you. Employee at $16 per hour, equals $4 for every 15 minutes so being late every day is $20/ week. Once a week 15-minute extra lunch that is now $24 a week. Add in 30 minutes a week leaving early that is an additional $8 so she was getting paid $32/week or $128/month or $1536 /year for doing NOTHING!

What about lost business? If your average sale is $80 and you lose *just* three of those per week, that is $240 x 52 weeks = $12,480! Can you afford to lose that?

Personally, I look at this as employee theft on more than one level! The business owner is not just paying the employee for not working, but there is significant lost revenue! However you look at it, it is lost money.

A business owner has the right to give time off to an employee with pay any time. Most employees love paid time off and that is a great benefit for you to provide them. However, you need to notice when it is not authorized. You also must incorporate a strategy for the allowed time off, so as not to miss out on potential revenue. Not to mention, sometimes when customers get angry after driving all the way to a business to find it closed, you can lose a customer forever. Giving your employees time off is a great way to keep good employees, but you need to figure out a way to cover that time so you don't lose revenue.

Here is another example of a client who lost a lot of money in an instant. My client, a chiropractor, "Andy", is a very good chiropractor but doesn't like the "business owner" part of the equation. That is unfortunate since he was very much in business. Andy had a receptionist, "Katie," who got into an altercation with a patient. Katie, told the patient she could not have what she wanted because that was the rule. The patient asked Katie to please check with Dr. Andy, but Katie refused. The rules were the rules and she did not need to ask anyone. Katie was very unprofessional and quite rude to the patient. The patient had been coming to Andy for years, along with several friends and family members who she had referred to Andy. Katie had the attitude towards the patient that her business did not matter and she told the patient that she was free to go elsewhere. Well, that is exactly what the patient did. And, even worse, she found a new chiropractor and her five friends and family members left and went to the new chiropractor as well.

Within 10 minutes, Andy lost six patients along with any future referrals. Andy was devastated. He lost thousands of dollars in business, not to mention patients he really enjoyed working with, all because of an unnecessary altercation with an untrained receptionist.

Has this ever happened to you? Do you even know if it has? You may not even know if this has happened in your business because not all customers will tell you. It is very possible that you have had employees who have conducted themselves in some way that has lost customers for your business.

This chapter is about numbers and revenue. However, I would like to take a moment to point out an issue that will be covered in a later chapter. Many small business owners either don't have the time, knowledge and/or resources to hire the right people and/or train their employees to prevent these things from happening. This is why every business owner truly needs someone they can work with, i.e., business coach or mentor, to get the resources you need. You cannot be a master of all parts of your business.

In this case, the chiropractor, Andy, is an exceptional doctor. Instead of reaching out for resources to hire and train his employees, he just hired people he thought would work out. Proper training was not provided as well.

You may or may not be great at hiring and training employees. Let's get back to the numbers and loss of possible revenue in your business. Define and recognize your areas of strengths and weaknesses.  Use your strengths to run your business.  Allow yourself to reach out to resources for help in the areas that are not your strengths.  This also helps you avoid tying up your valuable time and skills that should be directed to other areas of your business.  In this case, I did not recommend that Andy start getting training on how to hire employees, I recommended he seek help from someone to do the hiring for him.

In a future chapter, we will discuss how vital it is to have an employee manual, well-written job description and well-written expectations your employees.  Having these manuals will help keep you from the above situations and lost revenue.

It is very hard for small business owners to be able to "watch" what is going on at all times in their business.  There is also no one size fits all.  That is one good reason to have business coaches and consultants who are able to work with you, and even design workshops and trainings to fit YOUR needs specifically.  Good business coaches and consultants will give you the tools you need for YOUR business.  They also design strategies for your specific business to solve issues like what happened to Andy.

In Andy's case, we worked with him to get the right tools and now his business is back on track.  Our first action item was a meeting with Katie to discuss the situation.  She was put on notice and eventually let go.  After a short time, it became obvious Katie was not a good fit for the position and the position was not a good fit for her either.  We helped Andy to hire a new person, along with designing a very detailed employee manual, job descriptions and, expectations for a new hire.  Knowing the right questions to ask the prospective new hire worked to get the right person for the position. Having the resources to hire along with the employee manuals were the key for Andy! The new hire was required to read everything and agree to it by signing. She then had these tools to use on a daily basis to make sure she met the expectations of the business. No more lost revenue! Employees need clear direction. They need and want manuals, descriptions, expectations, etc., for them to be able to perform their best. Having these tools saves you time answering questions, which saves you money.

Over the years, I have encountered so many different scenarios in this area of how businesses have lost serious revenue and some without even realizing it. Just a few simple tools can prevent these types of scenarios from happening. Do realize though, that nothing in life is perfect. You can have all the tools in the world and in the right place, and still, every once in a while get that employee that seemed so awesome and turns out to be anything but awesome. After all, we are dealing with humans! If you have the right tools and direction, you can easily remedy the situations of those anything but awesome employees!

**Do you talk to your employees about the numbers for your business?** It is a very important thing to do. Some business owners are concerned about "letting their employees know their financial business". Some of the information regarding your business' numbers can be very important and advantageous to share with your employees. A good example is employees knowing your sales goals. In order for them to hit your revenue goals, the employees need to know what those goals are.

Involving your staff can make for better employees. First, ask your employees what their goals are. Ask them what kind of money they want to make and why. If they have a real why, they will have the drive for their why. Including the employee and their dreams will give them the drive that you need to grow your business. Think about it. If an employee sees a job with you as just trading time for money and no growth or incentive to reach their goals, why would they help you reach yours? They wouldn't. Do you blame them? You shouldn't. Most everyone has goals and dreams. Not to mention, how great would it feel if you were able to help your employees reach their goals and dreams?!

So, involve them. First, find out their needs, goals, dreams, and figure out how your business can help them achieve all of it. Then share with them what it will take for them to do in your business so that you can pay and/or promote them to the place they need to be in order to fulfill their goals. Win. Win. Yes, everybody wins. You win, because your employees are fulfilling their dreams (win) and fulfilling yours at the same time. Helping others to achieve their dreams is how you achieve yours. Some business owners don't think about that with employees. Time to give it a try, if you are not doing it already!

---

*Do you know what hidden expenses are in your business affecting your bottom line? Time to find out.*

---

**What about hidden revenue?** This one can be difficult to see. "Robert," who owned an HVAC company, wanted to go to the next level. They had maintenance agreements that they sold to customers. These maintenance agreements were great for the customer, as it kept their warranty valid. It also served as a money generator for the company. I noticed that they really weren't selling many and asked how they sold their maintenance agreements. Robert said they had their employees out in the field try to upsell them to the customers during installation. I had them start automatically putting the maintenance agreement in the original estimate for the new system. If the customer did not want it or could not afford it, fine. It could be removed from the estimate. But instead of trying to sell the maintenance agreement after the sale of the system, it is sold most often right up front! You are not forcing anyone to buy one but having it in the original sales contract will prompt the salesperson to educate the customer on why it is important to have. The next thing is to keep track of renewals and make sure you contact every customer for renewals. This added serious revenue!

This example can be done in any business that has an accessory, maintenance agreement and the like. If you automatically have it in your original price, no one will forget to inform the customer. There are many customers who would truly appreciate this, rather than later on wondering why no one told them about it.

"Jamie," who owns a flooring store, was looking for more ways to make money on what he was currently doing. He had a lot of floor cleaners sitting out in his showroom. I asked how many of those he sold. He said he was thinking of getting rid of them because sales were so low on them; they were just taking up valuable showroom space. When I asked Jamie how he sells the cleaners, he said that he recommends them to his customers and that was it. I asked him to try something different. I told him to give a bottle of floor cleaner to every customer who purchased a floor, at no charge. Also, let them know that it was so important to you that your customer's floor was properly maintained, that you were giving them the first bottle free. That floor cleaner turned out to be more revenue! The customers appreciated the free bottle and came in to purchase more when the bottles were empty! He added hundreds of dollars of monthly revenue to his store.

I call these "hidden" revenues because while they are not actually hidden, they are just little things that business owners don't always consider to add more revenue to their business. Usually, they are just thinking about more sales of their main product or service, forgetting that the little sales add up. Giving one bottle of floor cleaner away, sometimes resulted in selling a bottle to that customer every month. If you have 50 customers doing that, and you make $5 per bottle, you just added $250 per month to your revenue. Even better, you have people coming back to you on a regular basis, which keeps you on the top of their minds, which means more repeat business and referrals from them! If they are coming into your store every month or getting billed periodically for renewals of services, they won't forget about you and go anywhere else, thus better customer retention.

Again, some things seem insignificant, but they can lead to large sales.

Do you own the building where your business is located? Do you have extra space that is never used? You can lease this space to someone for their business or offer it as storage or office space. This space may not look very usable, but there are always people out there needing extra space for something. If you have an office that is very rarely used, you can rent it out on an as-needed basis. There are small businesses that do not need or cannot afford a fulltime office space. They would gladly pay a small price now and then to utilize your extra office when they need to meet with a client.

A lot of small businesses are very specialized and for a reason. They don't want to be a one-stop shop, they have their specialty product. However, it wouldn't hurt to take a look at adding something to compliment your main sales. If you own a dress shop, you certainly may not want to be a shoe store! However, what if you brought in one line of shoes that looked particularly awesome with your line of dresses? Or a specific line of scarves or jewelry? You are not creating a huge department store, but you are giving your customers an added value by saving them time going to another store, especially since you chose these items specifically for your main dress line. See if there is any item or service you may add to your business to add more revenue, without totally changing the main goal and purpose of your business.

There are thousands of hidden expenses and revenues because there are thousands of types of small businesses. This book will be a great guide in finding what is affecting your bottom line. You may need to dig even deeper. Mauri Consulting can work with you personally to get the best handle on your numbers.

## CHAPTER 5 -- DID YOU START YOUR BUSINESS ON THE RIGHT FOUNDATION?

Many business owners are having issues because they did not build the proper foundation for their businesses. Everything from the entity they started it on (i.e. sole proprietorship, corporation, etc.) to policies and procedures of the business. By the time they call me, they are in crisis mode. It is usually never too late, so don't worry.

> *Many entrepreneurs could have avoided the serious stress they are under by getting help when they first thought about opening up or buying a new business.*

They didn't, so here we are and ready to remedy the situations and get them on the right foot.

I cannot stress enough how important it is to start out on the right footing. I will not go into every detail here, as that is a whole book in and of itself.

For those of you who have a business idea, first, the chapter Know Your Why.

Get some help in deciding things like what entity type, sole proprietor, LLC, partnership, corporation, S-corporation and so forth.  Have a business plan.  A business plan needs to be in writing so you will actually follow it and do it!  Business plans can and most likely will change and evolve as time goes on, but you must start out with something to follow.

Instead of listing all the things that you need to get started,  I am going to give you some real life scenarios of small businesses who did not start out on the right footing.  If you already own a business, take a look at the foundation or footing that you started your business on.  If any of these scenarios remotely fit you or you believe that some of your issues may be the result of not starting out on the right footing, it is time to get some help on that.

 Let's talk about "Jerry" who owns a small plumbing company.  After working for a plumbing company for a number of years, Jerry decided to start his own.  He didn't start out on the right footing and didn't figure it out until about 20 years later.  Yes, that's right, 20 years later is when he finally realized that he had stayed in business, but had not started it out correctly.  This information is definitely for people at all stages of business.  Jerry proved that he could keep the doors open for 20 years, but was it really working?

Jerry was making a decent living.  Nothing luxurious, just making enough to take care of his family.  Jerry had been a sole proprietor all those years.  That would not be my choice, for sure, but that is what "he had always done".  While working with him, I heard "it's how I have always done it" about 100 times.  Remember, just because that is how you have always done it, and you managed to stay alive, doesn't mean it was the best way for you or your business.  Jerry never had a business plan, or a plan, period. He just went into business.

Now, Jerry wants to semi-retire and soon fully retire. He wants to turn the business over to his two children. I could write an entire book on this client and all of his scenarios, issues, and what we had to do to get him where he needed to be and is now. During most of what we had to do, he was kicking and screaming the whole way. However, as we made the changes, he saw a whole new light on his business and things are going so much better for his exit strategy!

The first issues we had to deal with were getting him out of sole proprietorship and changing his business to an S-Corp. He wanted to pass the business onto his children, but a sole proprietorship is just that "sole", only one person can own it. As the business sat, it could not be transferred to his children the way he wanted to, so he created an S-Corporation. This also took him from paying in thousands of dollars in income tax to a refund!

Another issue was revenue. He had been able to make it on the money he made. However, he wanted three people to survive from the income generated by this business. Jerry wanted some money coming to him for retirement and the two children wanted to make a living running the business. How do you take an income for one and make it into three? You have to increase the revenue! That is doable, but not an easy task and it won't happen overnight.

First, we had to get a plan on how this could happen and get it in writing so it would be followed. I noticed that he was not running the business on a percentage basis. As a numbers person, that made me cringe. So I asked him how he would calculate his estimates. He said he just "wings" it, and comes up with a price he thinks he can charge and make money. Wow, and he made it 20 years, amazing! That is not very typical. Well, Jerry wants to make a big change, and we have to prepare. We went over the numbers, as you read in the chapter, Know Your Numbers. Then we created a new procedure for estimating jobs after knowing the numbers. Within a short time of using the new way of estimating, and doing job costing, he increased his profit by 25%! He needed a lot more than that, but what a great start! He wasn't be able to retire as soon as he wanted to and his children had part time jobs to supplement their income until they could sustain a living on this business. Three years later, he is retired, receiving money and the children are making a good living from the business. Yes, a one family income, turned into a three-family income!

I need to mention that there are also people who buy businesses that were built on a solid footing, but they do not follow what the prior owners did to be successful. Here is a very sad story that happens all too often. This one did not end well. Unfortunately, this was not a client but the scenario of a man who bought an existing and successful business. I was sad to hear the story too late to be of help, as I found out at the very end. This scenario shows how important it is to keep your business on the right track and keep it on the solid foundation in which it was started.

"Zander" buys a business, actually what is called a "turnkey business". Creating a turnkey business is totally awesome and very profitable in selling and great for purchasing. Zander had worked in the industry of the business he purchased, so he had knowledge of the products and services.

This business was a solid turnkey business. The previous owner sold the business to Zander via owner financing, so that Zander could afford to buy the business. It is not always easy to get a loan for a business, so owner financing was great for Zander.

The business owner who sold the business to Zander told him, "This business is totally set up, all you need to do is follow what has been done and you will continue to do well and grow. DO NOT make any changes to the business until you have owned it for several years and are sure what changes to make. This year is the best year this business has ever had, you will do well, as long as you don't try to change it until you are ready, if ever."

What do you think was the first thing Zander did? Yep, he started making changes. Big changes. Expensive changes. He changed the people working there, changed the look, changed the website, changed the logo, changed the whole business model. Completely. For one thing, longtime customers are going to be leery of all these changes. The prior owner also told Zander "Do not make a big deal about me selling the business to you or me not being here anymore. Don't lie, but don't advertise it. I built this business on my reputation and my longtime customers may start looking elsewhere because you are an unknown. Don't make a big deal out of it until they have worked with you and are comfortable enough to stay." Good advice, if you ask me.

Well, you can guess what happened. Zander and his employees made a big deal about the old owner sold the business and moved away and the new owners were there. Yikes.

Another thing that went wrong was that Zander didn't know how to manage money. That business was making big money. The prior owner always kept a large amount in the bank account in order to have working capital for large jobs. The money was the first to go, well, for one thing, all those changes, they costed money.

Zander lost the business, had to file bankruptcy and a lot of people got hurt financially, including the prior owner who was not paid for their many years of blood, sweat, and tears to build the business, thinking this money would help them in retirement.

Here is a case where the business was started out on the right footing, but the new owner did not keep it there, thinking their changes would be better. The whole footing was demolished. Whether you start a business or buy one, the right footing matters and so does keeping the footing strong. Don't be Zander!

Zander could have kept this from happening he would have clearly defined his success and his why, he would have been driven to go forward successfully. If he had taken the time to know both of his business' numbers and the numbers he needed for his goals, he would not have spent all the money needed to run the business. The purpose of purchasing a turnkey business is so that you do not have to reinvent the wheel. Zander should have stuck to the existing business operations and not made changes until the appropriate timing. And last, but not least, if Zander had found a business coach at the beginning to help him with all of the above, he would be thriving today.

One thing commonly overlooked by small business owners are policy and procedure manuals, as well as how-to manuals for the work to be done in their business. Some have told me that it wasn't on their minds because they were so small, maybe one or two employees and that they figured they would just train verbally.

Policy and Procedure manuals are a must. It doesn't matter what size your business is. There are a lot of purposes for having this manual. For one, it sets the ground rules for your business. This is very important. It can be a lifesaver in the unfortunate event that you have to use disciplinary action or terminate someone's employment. If there is nothing in writing for policies for your business, then what policies are they in violation of?

A Policy and Procedure Manual should be written in detail from open to close and after closing and everything in between. Every task that is required of employees, along with your employment rules, i.e., hours and days they are expected to work; how many days can they be out sick; vacation time; customer service policies and so on.

Until you get management people on board (if you want to grow to that point), you will be doing the training. Some people remember everything you tell them, most don't. You can go over the manual with the new employee, and after that, they need to refer to it for reference on the job. It saves you time repeating yourself. As a busy small business owner, you may not even remember everything and they will not get all of the information they need to begin with.

Other manuals, if applicable, should be written and available to the employees as well. Depending on your business, you may have a lot of details an employee must know to do their job. Especially salespeople. And most especially salespeople when a service is involved! The salesperson must know everything they possibly can about the product and/or service you sell. In most businesses, they will not learn all of this on the first day. Would you rather your employee tells a customer, "I am not sure, let me look that up and get the correct answer". Or would you rather they keep asking you? Or, worse yet, would you rather they just "winged" an answer? I know as both a business owner and a customer, I am pretty impressed when an employee will say, "I am not sure, but I would be happy to find out", or "I am new here, I will have to look that up and get the correct information", and so on. That is much more impressive than an employee running back to the boss five times or winging it and giving me an incorrect answer!

As a business owner, there is nothing more frustrating than getting interrupted by employees asking me a million questions. In my businesses, I designed and wrote a policy and procedure manual, along with manuals for just about everything in that business. I get very, very few interruptions from employees and my customers always get correct answers. Not to mention, there are times when I cannot be in that location and possibly unreachable. The business cannot just stop because I am not available to answer a question. The business needs to keep moving smoothly, with or without my presence.

When customers see you grab a book or a binder to look up an answer to the question, it enhances your credibility. They see something in writing, not just an answer off the top of someone's head. It may take a couple minutes, but believe me, the customer is happy that the employee is resourceful! It leaves no doubt in their mind that they got the correct information. Put everything in those manuals. I mean everything. You may think that some small piece of information is "common sense" or juvenile, but it is not. Every detail about how your business is to be run is important.

If you are not sure how to do an employee manual, job descriptions and other manuals that should be used in your business, hire it out. It is too critical to put off and/or not do at all.

## CHAPTER 6 - WHY YOU SHOULD TRACK YOUR BUSINESS AND HOW

It is so important to track where your business comes from.

> *When you know where the majority of your business comes from, it helps you to know where and how to market.*

I have worked with many small businesses that do not track how their customers find them. Some thought it wasn't important and others had tons of excuses why not to track.

There are many small businesses that are spending a lot of time marketing and money on advertising that isn't working for their business at all, and they don't even know why. There are a lot of reasons for this, some do not know their target market, some do not know the ROI (return on investment) for marketing and advertising and more.

So far, I have not found a business that was unable to find a way to track their business. I have worked with retail businesses that say they are so busy waiting on the customers, how would they have time. Well, you can't afford not to. It only takes one second to ask "How did you find us?" or "How did you hear about us?" and jot it down when it is convenient, but the sooner the better so you do not forget. If you have a cash register with employees ringing up sales, put a notebook or sheet of paper on the counter with columns. The paper could look something like this:

| Walk In | Referred by customer | Coupon | Social Media | TV | Radio | Other |
|---|---|---|---|---|---|---|
|  |  |  |  |  |  |  |
|  |  |  |  |  |  |  |
|  |  |  |  |  |  |  |
|  |  |  |  |  |  |  |

Have the employee put a mark in each category as they get the information from the customer. If a customer mentioned a particular customer's name, put that on the sheet and keep track of how many customers are referred by each existing customer.

If you create invoices for your customers and use an accounting program, such as QuickBooks, you can track on each invoice how they found you. What is great about that, you can do a report which will show numbers, percentages, and graphs of where your business is coming from.

There is so much you can do with this information. You will know what advertising works, how well it works or doesn't, who your biggest fans are and more. You can use the data to create target marketing, along with contests and more.

Here is a real-life example. A client, "Susie," was spending a ton of money every month on radio advertising, but she was struggling and could no longer afford it. Some businesses work well with radio, some don't. It depends on the type of business, location, listeners, so many variables. I asked her how much she was paying for the radio and how much business she was getting from those ads. All Susie knew was that it was costing her $1800.00 per month for the ads and no clue if she got any business from it. I got her to start tracking immediately. After 90 days, we took a look at where her customers were coming from. She had been on the radio for a year. During that ninety days, not one customer found her from the radio ad. In fact, 50% of her business was coming from prior customers, 20% was walk-in (they just saw her place of business), 10% was from a networking group she had joined a few months ago, 8% was from looking up her products/services online and the last 12% were repeat customers.

Wow, that was serious eye-opening information for Susie. Imagine if she had been doing this tracking the entire time she was in business! Her particular industry was not a good fit for radio, as the ROI was zero at this point. Take a look at the big one, the 50%, which is referrals from prior customers! She had no clue because she had never asked! Now, what is she going to do? Well, first of all, Susie kept on tracking all of her business. She started contacting her current customers in various ways to get more referrals and more repeat business. She upped her involvement in the networking group, which brought in even more business from the group.

Over the next several months, she gained even more knowledge of where her customers came from and started taking action. Her business revenue went up 40%! Imagine that, taking that extra few seconds with each customer to ask how they found her business, and taking that information and growing their revenue by 40%! Not to mention, ditching the advertising that had no ROI for her.

Now, I want to make something clear. I am not saying anything negative about radio advertising!! I am not negative about any type of advertising, but it has to be the right fit for the business and if there is no ROI, then you need to stop, no matter what type of advertising it is. This is just one specific business's example.

If she would have found that most of her customers were finding her from the radio, then by all means, she would have stayed with it and even added more airtime. Or if another method of advertising was working, then should could have stick with that. If it works for your business, do it. If it doesn't, then stop. The only way to know is by tracking where your business comes from.

There is a lot you can do once you have these numbers, some of which will be covered in later chapters.

# CHAPTER 7 --WHAT FEARS ARE HOLDING YOUR BUSINESS BACK

Most people have some sort of fear with their businesses. Sometimes business owners have fears they don't even realize that hold them back from growing or succeeding in business. We will start with some common fears.

**Fear of failure.** This is one of the most common fears I hear. First of all, failure means something different to everyone. Failure may mean that the business falls apart and you have to shut it down. In that case, fear of bankruptcy, loss of reputation, and fear of looking inadequate to others may creep into your mind. Your friends and family may have told you that you couldn't run your own business, or shouldn't because you may fail. You may fear not meeting the expectations of others. The fear list goes on.

It is true when starting up a business, you must be willing to take a leap of faith. There are no guarantees. And circumstances beyond control definitely do happen, i.e. a very small business where the business revolves around the owner being there at all times and they have a tragedy in their lives.

---

*When starting up a business, you must be willing to take a leap of faith!*

---

Most small businesses, if run properly, should be able to make it through good times and tough times. There are a number of reasons why people don't ask for help. Fear of rejection; they don't want to appear stupid; they worry it will undermine their achievements; they don't want people to know they are struggling. The reality is, very few people achieve great success without the support and assistance of others. Often people are willing to help if you just reach out and ask them.

If you are struggling, this book and our workshops are intended to help get you back on your feet. The key is to reach out for help before it is too late. When things are going well, or even just OK, most people just keep on going and do not reach out for any kind of assistance. Most of the people who do not reach out are the ones that have been in business the longest or are of a certain age. For some reason, they seem to think that they will look bad for reaching out to business coaches, workshops, mentors, friends, etc., for help. It is actually quite the opposite.

No matter your age or experience, no one knows it all and the business world is everchanging! No matter what you think, you can always learn from others. You may think you know it all or have been doing it long enough that you don't need any further education of any kind, but that is setting yourself up for possible failure!

Get rid of the fear of failing by making sure you seek out the right information to start your business correctly and continue seeking the right information to keep you going in good times and in bad.

As mentioned earlier, there is no one-size-fits all in business. This book is intended to help as many small businesses as possible. You will definitely want to check out our workshops to see how else we can serve you, along with our coaching programs, masterminds, and workshops designed for you specifically.

Do not stress yourself with fear of failing. Get the guidance you need!

You can also use your fear to motivate you! Instead of focusing on the possibility of failing, focus on the positive outcome of success! You will always have small failures in business. You will try things and they won't work out the way you planned. Get up and dust yourself off, figure out another angle. Sometimes failures turn into something spectacular because you came up with a new idea that was phenomenal for your business when a different idea failed to work!

**Do you really know the consequences of failing?** Are the consequences really that bad? For many who have this fear of failure, the impact of failure would often be negligible—maybe a little bit of embarrassment, possibly a waste of time and/or resources.

To get over the fear of failure, ask yourself, "So, what if I do fail?" What is the worst that can happen? Make a list of all the consequences of any failures that could happen in your business. If the reality is "Not a lot," which is often the case with my coaching clients, give it a shot. What do you really have to lose?

**Cold calling!** This is a very common fear for most people, period. There are a lot of businesses that may need to call people they don't know to get business. This is especially true in the startup phase.

For example, a new ad agency just opened, and it has no clients. The business owner will either need to go out to businesses and talk to them or call them on the phone. He or she can send an email or utilize direct mailing as well. No matter what method they use, it is all classified as "cold calling." This can be one of the most difficult and scary things to do in business.

There are some people who love to go out and meet people and call people, they are totally "people" people! They love it and are good at it. However, even outgoing people who love to meet new people can have a hard time with cold calling.

Why is it so scary? One reason is because the definition of fear is "an unpleasant emotion caused by the belief that someone or something is dangerous, likely to cause pain or a threat." Three of the biggest fears of cold calling is rejection and/or looking inadequate in someone's eyes and failure (hearing the word no). Therefore, fear of cold calling is actually the unknown outcome or response. Yes, sometimes there are less than desirable outcomes from calling someone you don't know and asking them for something. It will happen. Or will it? Actually, what you're *feeling* is really the only fearful part of the outcome. You see, if someone says no to what you are asking, you may *feel* a certain way. For example, you may feel like a failure because they said no. You take it personally.

First of all, it is not personal; it is business. Either the person on the other end wants your product or service or they don't. They either need your product or service or they don't. It is not you they don't want. If you are professional, polite, and respectful when calling or meeting someone, you are doing all you can do. Obviously, if you are unprofessional, rude, disrespectful, then, sorry it is you and you are in the wrong profession. That is most likely not the case for you.

There are several ways to get over the "fear" of cold calling. Here are some tips for calling prospective customers on the phone.

- Stand up. It is so much easier to have courage when standing, then when sitting.
- Walk around while you talk.
- Start with a smile on your face. People can "hear" your smile. They can hear your energy, low or high.
- When you dial the number, think about this person as a friend of yours, someone you really like and respect. Speak to the prospect like you would speak to someone in your life that you like and respect.
- Be happy and upbeat, this is just a person, like you, no one extra special, just another human being.

It really does help to smile, stand and walk around. It projects your voice better and it makes you feel more comfortable. Sitting at a desk is boring and makes it hard to sound excited.

They can't hurt you over the phone. No matter how they react, it will only hurt you if you let it. If you can pick up the phone and order a pizza, make reservations, or talk to your friends, you can call anyone. You have to look at them as just another person in this world, who may be just as nervous about answering that call as you are making the call!

Keep in mind that you need no's. You don't want all yes's! That will come in a later chapter, but for now, you just need to know that you don't want everyone to be your customer.

Also, in life, you can't know what it is truly like to have success without failure. After having some no's, those yes's will feel great!

**Fear of having to meet someone in person.** Make sure you look good because you will feel good and have more confidence. Be professional, but also try to be comfortable. Walk into a business with the mindset that you are a customer rather than them being a prospective customer! Yes, that will set you more at ease. If you think of them as an equal, instead of them being in control of your emotions, your fear will go away. Be excited to be there. Be excited to see what they do and the fact that you may actually become friends with someone there. Learn about them and their business first, then educate them about what you do. Go in with an attitude that you want to know all about them and have the opportunity to educate them about your passion. See the chapter Sales is Not About "Selling" How to Get Sales Without "Selling." You are just there to educate them on what you have and let them decide if they need your product/service.

**There is also a fear of going to the next level.** It can be tricky when you are at the stage where you need to hire more people to handle the work, but the money just isn't there yet. It is a really tough place to be stuck in. Depending on your business, you have to look at it like this: Will hiring another person add more revenue? If yes, then take the leap and hire that person. It may seem like you cannot afford it, but if they are going to bring in more revenue, yes it may be tight at first, but how will you get that extra revenue without them?

You may be doing all the bookkeeping for your business and just can't handle working 20 hours a day anymore, but feel you cannot afford a bookkeeper. Take a look at your numbers and your time. What would you be doing if you weren't doing the bookkeeping? Would you be doing something that would be increasing revenue in your business? Then hire someone to do the bookkeeping! What if you pay the part-time bookkeeper a couple hundred dollars a month, but you turn around with that free time and bring in $5000 a month?! Look carefully at your numbers and business model and see if this is what might happen.

You may also be afraid of your company growing and wondering if you are able to handle the growth. Maybe you fear being overwhelmed. The best way to handle this fear is to do some real soul searching and goal searching! What do you really want? Go back to your passion, dreams, and goals, the why for your business. Do you need your business to go to that level for you to achieve your goals? Maybe you don't.

It is OK to get to a certain point with your business and not grow any larger, as long as you have achieved the dreams you desire, and stay there. Not everyone's dreams require for their business to be the largest or several locations. When you are happy with where you are, do not feel you have to go to the next level.

If you need to get to the next level in order to achieve your dreams, then keep focused on your why and your passion. Keep focused on what your success will look like. Make a plan. What do you need to do to reach that next level. If you feel you cannot handle the extra work you perceive because of the growth, take a look at what the extra work would actually become. In the plan, calculate the numbers, time and what it would take to handle that next level. It would be a good idea to work with a business coach on this to make sure that your transition to this new level is smooth.

**Fear of not being able to take time away from your business.** One of the best things for you and your business is to make sure to take time off! You need vacation time to rejuvenate and refresh yourself. How can you be the best visionary and leader for your business, if you don't take care of yourself?!

You should never make your entire business revolve around your efforts only. Set the business up with a plan for hiring people to take over certain jobs to alleviate time from you. Delegate duties to the right people. It is critical that you get time off. What good does it do to make great money if you never take the time to enjoy the fruits of your labor?

Today, it is easier than ever to keep in touch with your business. If you don't feel you can leave for a vacation and go off the grid, then take a couple of days rest at home by keeping the contact with your employees to a minimum. Make a list of what could really go wrong without you being there. Would it really be that bad if a few mistakes were made? Who knows, your people may surprise you and take excellent care of your business while you are gone! That means you are a great leader and trained them properly! If not, then you need to change your mindset and leadership skills.

Making yourself indispensable at your company is a huge mistake. It will literally take life away from you. Put the right policies and procedures in place and hire the right people. Lead your people. Remember, life happens. People who make themselves indispensable (or believe they are), never leave their business, and they don't think of the possibility of a catastrophic event which could take them away from their business outside of their control. You are afraid to leave, but what if you were in an accident or had an illness, or something happened to a loved one and you had no choice but to be gone from your business, say for a month or two?

Quit being afraid of what might happen if you leave your business. Instead, put the right people in the right positions and have the right policies and procedures in place!

## CHAPTER 8-- IS THE CUSTOMER ALWAYS RIGHT?

This is a question of concern for so many business owners. Years, ago, some of the large department stores started this mantra: "The Customer is Always Right." Think about that for a minute. First of all, is anyone on this earth always right? I think not. My answer to the question, "Is the Customer Always Right?" is no.

You may think this chapter is for customers, rather than business owners. Well, in fact, I wish every person who buys anything would read this! On the flip side, all business owners are also consumers!

Ok, I get it, businesses want to make their customers happy and have them come back. It is all about treating them right. I get it. However, the customer is not always right, and in some instances it can be very bad for your business to operate with that mindset.

Difficult customers are a fact of life for every company. Assuming they're always right could destroy your business. One of the more difficult truths to accept is that some customers aren't a good fit for your brand, and you can't realize that until you accept that they aren't always right.

> *The customer is not always right, and in some instances, it can be very bad for your business to operate with that mindset.*

This doesn't mean that the customer is never right or that you can't learn anything from customer feedback. On the contrary, that feedback is still vital to any company's growth and success.

However, it's time for companies, especially very small businesses, to let go of the myth that appeasement equals customer satisfaction and loyalty. Only then can they finally focus on providing customers with the products, services, and experiences they'll truly appreciate.

There are many ways where having the "customer is always right" attitude and business practice can be harmful.

It is mostly about promises and expectations. In the very beginning, you must inform customers of what they can expect and be totally honest about it. Never promise a customer anything that you personally cannot guarantee, especially when a third party is involved.

Here is a classic example. Your customer wants to purchase a product you have to order and they want it by a certain date. This could go two ways, one with the customer being right and one with the customer not being right. You tell the customer that the product will definitely be here on the date they requested because after all, the manufacturer and shipping company said it would be. Something goes wrong and the product does not show up on that day. The customer is angry because you promised them it would be there on time. The customer is right and the complaint is valid.

Scenario number two. You explained to the customer that the product "should" be here on a certain date, according to the manufacturer and shipper, **however**, you also explain to them with certainty that the item may not be there on time. You go on to let them know that you are not in control of the manufacturer or the shipper. You cannot be 100% certain that the employees of the manufacturer will get it to the shipping facility immediately and that there will not be any delays in the shipping. A wise idea would be to write this information on the receipt, to stop a "he said, she said" situation if things don't turn out correctly.

Now assume the product does not come in on time. The customer is angry, complaining, and wanting a discount. Is the customer right? No. Their expectations were higher than you promised. How you handle it from here is also important. You don't want to be snippy and say "Well, I told you..." because, of course, no one likes to be "told" or given an, "I told you so." You need to very politely and professionally apologize it did not make it on time, empathize with them and gently remind them that you are not in control of other people or businesses. Let them know that the minute the product is received, they will get a call.

In the latter situation, the customer is not right. Either they were not paying attention to what you explained to them, did not read the receipt, or just plain ignored it. Why would they ignore it? Because all we have heard for years is that the customer is always right no matter what. There are a lot of people who abuse it to get their way or get a discount or something free. No one can control other people or businesses. However, it is on you to never make a promise or guarantee you cannot keep.

Even it if is a service that you provide and you know you can be there on that day, it is unwise to promise and/or guarantee that you can do it. Life happens. Not too long ago, I had some deadlines that I was sure I could make. I woke up one day and needed to be rushed to the ER. One emergency surgery, a 10-day hospital stay, and many weeks of recovery later, I was back to my work. Luckily for me, the clients were understanding. Did I have any clue that was going to happen to me? Of course not! It shows you, though, that anything unexpected can happen at any time. It is best to never absolutely promise anything. Always say that you will do whatever you possibly can to make it happen, but that something could interfere with that plan because you cannot control life.

The majority of people are honest and are not out to hurt anyone, especially intentionally. However, there are some people out there that are not honest and will lie, cheat and steal, sometimes just for the fun of it. Let's face it, we do not live in a perfect world.

Buyer's remorse is a real thing as well. Dishonest people are out there too. I truly hate being negative, but there are times when you have to bring up negative situations so that you can learn from it and use it to keep your business from harm.

"Jamie" owns a flooring store and installed $30,000 worth of flooring in a lady's home. She came into the store during the process and mentioned to Jamie that her mom told her she had no business spending that kind of money on flooring as a single mom. Jamie didn't think anything of it. When the job was done and Jamie went to collect the remaining $7,000, the lady said she wasn't going to pay because the job was not done properly, and she wasn't happy. Jamie set up an appointment to go to her house to find out what was wrong with the job. When he got there, she went on and on about the wood being too dark for her house and it looked like a dungeon in her house and she just wasn't happy. Before the job started, the customer had picked out the wood after taking several samples home to see how they would look in her house. After making all of her choices for the job, she signed a contract which clearly stated her choices.

The customer showed Jamie a couple of areas where they had missed putty on nail holes on the trim boards. He said he would get his guy right out there to put the putty in those few holes. He set up a time for later that day for this to be done. She agreed on the time. When the installer got to her house, she would not let him the house. They made another appointment for a week later and she let the installer in and he filled the holes. Jamie asked for his final balance due to him. She said "No, I cannot live with the color of this floor. I will not pay you until you replace it with a different color."

It ended up going to court. After a good bit of money spent, Jamie won. But Jamie really didn't really "win." True, he won the court case. But, he actually lost, due to court costs, costs of his time, and costs of his employee's time going to court.

Was the customer right? No. Just because the customer isn't happy, does not mean they are right. This customer, in my opinion, was suffering from buyer's remorse. She did not want to pay the final balance because she felt she should not have spent the money in the first place. Well, I am sorry, but that is on her. She picked out the color, signed the contract, and the job was done correctly. So why should she not pay? It would have cost Jamie a fortune out of his own pocket to replace that floor and his business would have seriously gone in the hole if he had replaced the flooring. As it was, he lost most, if not all of his profit going to court. However, he lost a lot less by going to court and he did not give in to the buyer's remorse.

I have worked with business owners who have had the belief that the customer is always right, and it has cost them big time! They have actually caved in to people like the lady mentioned above, because they thought they had to. They were worried about their reputations. If Jamie had replaced that floor, he would have shown everyone that he can be cheated. There are major department stores who have had the stance that the customer is always right, and they will take anything back just to make the customer happy. I don't know about you, but over the years, I have seen many people buy something, use it once and then return it and get their money back. They only needed that dress for a day or that appliance for one event, and so on. Maybe the big box stores can afford to do that, however, doesn't that just drive up the prices for everyone else when they lose that money? They certainly cannot, (definitely should not) sell a used item as new, so what happens to the item?

That way of thinking came from the big box stores many years ago and has trickled down to some of the small businesses. Unfortunately, some shoppers out there take this saying quite seriously and some use it to their advantage. They don't think about the fact that it hurts anyone, and actually, it hurts them in the long run when prices go up.

Do not let the customer take advantage of you! You don't have to. If your business is run honestly and legitimately, and you explain clearly upfront what you really are able to promise or not promise, it should be a moot point.

**Another way to look at "the customer is always right" is how hard it is on your employees.** Your employees will possibly take serious abuse from customers who are always right! It also can be demoralizing.

"Tony", a painter, was given a paint sample by his customer to get paint mixed and paint two rooms. Tony took the sample to the paint store, had it mixed, and it was identical to the sample. The customers were at work and left Tony a key. He was to go in and paint while they were gone. He painted the two rooms and left for the day. He received a phone call that evening from the lady, who was distraught, telling Tony that he had to get different paint and repaint the rooms. He asked why, what was wrong with the paint job? She said the color is not what she expected it to look like. She also said, "I expect you to do this on your own dime because it is not what I wanted." Tony mentioned to her that she gave him the color sample and it was what she wanted. She said, "Yeah, but once you put it on the walls, couldn't you see how pink it was?!" He said, "Of course, but how did I know you did not want pink?" He went ahead and repainted at no charge. Big mistake. He not only lost money, but he showed this lady that she could take advantage of him.

"Amanda" owns a carpet cleaning business. One of her employees went out to clean carpets for a customer. The customer was very rude to the employee and wanted more work done than she had paid for. The employee followed orders from his boss and did what was on his work order. He told the customer that if she wanted more services, it would cost more money. He said he would be happy to provide the extra services if she would sign a form accepting the amount. She would not so he did not do any more than his work order stated. After the employee left, the customer called Amanda and complained that she did not get what she wanted. Unfortunately, Amanda had the "customer is always right" attitude and sent another employee out there to give her what she wanted, and free of charge. She also apologized profusely.

Amanda's actions belittled her loyal employee. She made it look like her employee was wrong. Her employee actually had her back by not giving out more service than what was paid for and asking the customer to pay for additional services. Look at what this cost Amanda! I worked with Amanda to address her business philosophy. She changed her attitude and started firing some of her undesirable customers. Amanda's revenue and profit went up soon after!

Keep in mind that like-minded people do hang out together. Just think what could happen if a customer like her tells all their like-minded friends how they can get free services out of your business if they just complain (even if it is not warranted). Not good for business.

This is also not fair to your valued paying customers. They are paying full price and not getting any extras because they are good and loyal customers.

Customer service is so important in your business. You need to treat your customers right to keep them and get referrals. You also need to know which customers to let go. You don't want every customer!

Here is an experience I had many years ago that will stick with me forever. It happened in one of my flooring stores. One of my biggest personal challenges was that I always wanted to please 100% of my customers 100% of the time. One day a real nice gentleman came into my store and signed a contract to get some flooring done in his home. As always, I wanted that job to go perfectly, but it didn't. There was an issue with the materials and I had to contact the customer to let him know there was a problem and what we needed to do to resolve it. It took some time and was agonizing for me to inconvenience this man, but finally, the project was completed and all was well.

When the man came in to pay his final bill, I again apologized profusely for the inconvenience. Here is what he said to me. They were words I will never forget, and wish every customer would hear and repeat. He said, "I work hard for my money and this floor cost me a good bit of my hard-earned dollars. However, it is just a floor. You see, my wife was killed at the Pentagon on 9-11. This, this is just a floor. It can be fixed.

Nothing will bring my wife back. In the grand scheme of life, this is just a thing, so don't stress over it because I am not stressing over it." I almost started bawling. It took all I muster to keep my composure. There had been a few times when something had to be fixed and the customer treated my employees like they were going to die because of it. Some actually portrayed extreme and inappropriate rudeness over a very fixable issue. All because they were "inconvenienced." Well, life is full of inconveniences, and while as business owners, we work very hard not to inconvenience anyone, it happens.

I wish everyone could look at all products and services the way that particular customer did. Think about it, what is most important in life? I know that people work hard for their money and want to get the most out of that hard-earned money. I also know that there are some bad business owners out there, just like every single profession. There are good and bad people everywhere. The majority of small business owners are decent hardworking people. Remember though, they are human and so are their employees. Humans make mistakes. Most often whatever product or service they buy is not life-threatening. The world will not end because they did not get the product or service on time, or exactly the way they wanted it.

What really matters, is how the situation is handled. If the business does everything they can to correct the mistake and resolve the issue for the customer, that is most important. Business owners are also customers. Be that customer that doesn't make not getting the perfect product a life-ending matter. Pass that information on to your customers as well. Obviously, you want to say it in a tactful way. If everyone had the attitude my customer did, what a happier world it would be, wouldn't it?

In summary, no, the customer is not always right. Be very aware of when they are and when they are not by explaining what they can expect and not over-promising.

## CHAPTER 9 – WHY YOU NEED OTHERS

Business coaches provide accountability. They serve your business by developing strategies and plans to grow your business. Since there is no "one size fits all", business coaches tailor strategies to the specific goals for you and your business. The coach is there to keep track and measure progress that someone might avoid recording if they are on their own.

Many great small business owners credit their success in part to having a great business coach. I certainly do.

> *Having great coaches and participating in mastermind groups helped my business grow considerably.*

Business Coaches/Consultants. No matter how long you have been in business and how good you are at it, you will never, and I mean never, know it all. If you show me a person on this earth who knows absolutely everything, I'll show you a person who still has a lot to learn. There is no such thing on this earth as a perfect person. We are all "works in progress" our entire lives. Hopefully, the older we get the more experienced and wiser we are, but we will never know it all, no matter how hard we try or "think" we do!

A nice thing about a business coach is that they do not work in your business! They are on the outside looking in. You know how easy it is to see problems in other peoples' lives and businesses? It is not, however, so simple to see it in your own life/business. It never is. Just like pointing out other people's faults is so much easier than pointing out your own. I am not saying you need a coach because you are making mistakes. There is always room to learn. Maybe there are hidden expenses or revenues that you are not seeing. Maybe there is room for improvement in the infrastructure of your business. Your business may need foundation repairs. You may be stuck and need help with a strategy to get unstuck and move to the next level. Maybe you are not getting to the next level, because there are just a couple of things that need to be tweaked in your business, or you need a detailed plan.

It might be the right time to plan your exit strategy. This is critical. There is nothing worse than being ready to retire, hoping to have money from your blood, sweat, and tears, and not being able to get there.

Maybe you are on the verge of closing the doors and need a strategy to keep from losing your business. No matter what stage or state your business is, you will always benefit from an outside coach to take a look at things.

Interview this coach. Ask them a lot of questions. Buy some of their workshops or their book, etc., to see what their style is. Make sure your personalities work well together. Nowadays people are so busy and because we have the technology available, you don't even have to leave your office or have them come to you. Most things can be done via phone, email, video conferencing and more. Regardless, it is very important to your business.

Questions you should ask a business coach:
- Have you ever owned a business?
- How many and what type of businesses have you owned?
- What experience do you have in starting, purchasing, operating and selling businesses?
- What areas of business are you most experienced?
- Will you design strategies for my business?
- Do you hold your clients accountable?
- What is expected of me in your processes?
- 

If you are low on funds, rather than doing a one-on-one consulting, buy and download their online workshops or see if they have local workshops/seminars you can attend. It is generally much less expensive to join a group setting or buy workshops online than one on one services. This is a great way to get the information inexpensively. Most will answer follow up email questions you may have regarding their workshops. Today, with life being so busy, it may be easier for you to do a workshop online and communicate with a coach via email. During the day, there are many distractions. It may be much easier for you to get this help after hours.

Mentors are great too. Mentors are usually people in your life, profession, etc., that know you and that you trust. These people help guide you in an industry with some of their experiences. Having a mentor is a great feeling of security at times. If you are in a jam and need immediate advice, call a mentor if you believe they can help. Generally, someone who takes on the role of being your mentor is someone that cares about your wellbeing. They may not have all of the answers and will refer you to an expert who does, but they have your best interest at heart and will give you great moral support.

A mastermind group is a peer-to-peer mentoring concept used to help members solve their problems with input and advice from the other group members. The concept was coined in 1925 by author Napoleon Hill in his book The Law of Success, and described in more detail in his 1937 book, Think and Grow Rich. In his books, Hill discussed the idea of the Master Mind, which referred to two or more people coming together in harmony to solve problems. (Wikipedia.org)

Cooperation through the use of mastermind groups was one of the laws of success that Hill learned studying successful Americans including Henry Ford, Thomas Edison, Alexander Graham Bell, Theodore Roosevelt, John D. Rockefeller, and Charles M. Schwab. (Wikipedia.org)

A mastermind group is essential to business owners and high-level management jobs. Usually, a mastermind group is 6-10 people who are all business owners or people in high-level management positions. You need at least 6 people in order to have enough ideas, but no more than 10 or it will be too much. Business owners use masterminds because when you own the business, there is no one above you in the company to help you with issues. A peer group with people from all different types of businesses with various backgrounds get together and solve problems for each other. If you are in management, you may still be in the predicament that you have no one to work with to solve problems. Join a mastermind with other managers and share and learn! And in life in general, it is awesome to have a group of people you can get together with once a month, once a week, etc. to do problem-solving! In your personal life, maybe you want to grow in an area of your life. There are other people out there that want the same thing, we can set up a mastermind for any area of your life!

It is key to find a very good facilitator who holds masterminds. Usually, after about a year or so, the group goes on without a facilitator. The facilitator should be someone who is in the business coaching or consulting industry. They are responsible for vetting the businesses, making sure the right people are meeting together (personality, professions, level/stage of business etc.). It is important to put the right people together in a mastermind or it will not be successful. The facilitator helps design the agenda and keeps the group moving forward with that agenda.

With a good facilitator and a good bunch of small business owners, a mastermind will definitely help you get to the next level in your business! It is an incredible learning and problem-solving experience for any business owner at any stage in their business.

Mauri Consulting is a company focused on serving others. Our passion is sharing tools and information for you to acquire your goals and dreams. One of our most popular tools is our "Pay it Forward Business Method." We believe "A Pure Giving Heart = SUCCESS"! Success varies from person to person, so success for one person is far different than it is for another. How serious are you about achieving success in your life and business? Join us and we will empower you to fly to the next level!

www.MauriConsulting.com

Mauri Consulting Offers:
- Specific Workshops, Seminars, and Trainings
- Online Courses and Workshops
- Facilitation and Mentoring Mastermind Groups
- Individual Consulting, Training, and Workshops
- Service of Others
- Empowering of Communities

Contact us at info@mauriconsulting.com<br>www.mauriconsulting.com

Like and follow us on Facebook<br>https://www.facebook.com/mauriconsulting/

Please email and inform us how this book worked for you. In fact, email us periodically and let us know what you have tried, how well it worked, and what level you gained. We would love hear from you!

Copyright 2019. All Rights Reserved.

www.ingramcontent.com/pod-product-compliance
Lightning Source LLC
Chambersburg PA
CBHW030950240526
45463CB00016B/2328